"*Love is patient, love is kind. It does not envy, it does not boast, it is not proud. It does not dishonor others, it is not self-seeking, it is not easily angered, it keeps no record of wrongs. Love does not delight in evil but rejoices with the truth. It always protects, always trusts, always hopes, always perseveres.*"

1 CORINTHIANS 13:4-7

Copyright · Imprint

Sacred Deposits™ · The Couples Workbook

"Where your treasure is, there your heart will be also."

— MATTHEW 6:21 (NIV)

THIS WORKBOOK BELONGS TO

HIS NAME

HER NAME

WEDDING DATE

CLASS / FACILITATOR

WE ARE OPENING THIS WORKBOOK BECAUSE:

OUR PRAYER FOR THIS SEASON

How To Use This Workbook

This workbook is the companion to *Sacred Deposits: The 5:1 Blueprint for Protecting Your Marriage*. Read the assigned chapters first. Then work the session. The system works when you work the system.

THREE WAYS TO ENGAGE

Path One

Personal Reflection

One chapter per week. Covenant Ledger Check individually. Your deposits do not require your spouse's participation.

Path Two

Couples Reset

Read together. Share answers as confession, not accusation. Begin the 30-Day Reset at Chapter 15.

Path Three

Group Study

Church groups, marriage retreats. One chapter per session. Licensing: contact@eqgenix.com

FIVE - PART SESSION STRUCTURE

1 BEFORE WE MEET

Read assigned chapters. Complete private reflection individually. Do not compare answers beforehand.

2 ACCOUNT HEALTH ASSESSMENT

Individual rating exercise. Designed to give you data about where the account actually is, not where you wish it were.

3 IN THE ROOM TOGETHER

Three to six discussion questions per session. Honest conversation, not performance. Say the hard thing.

4 THIS WEEK IN THE ACCOUNT

Three specific deposit practices before the next session. These are not optional.

5 COVENANT DECLARATION

Both partners sign at the close of each session. Eight sessions = eight signed declarations.

Session Map

Eight sessions aligned to the four parts of Sacred Deposits

PART ONE — THE FOUNDATION | *SESSION 1-2*

SESSION 1 — **The Account** — 8
Introduction + Ch 1–2 · The Covenant Exchange Rate™

SESSION 2 — **Emotional Safety** — 14
Ch 3–4 · The Brain, the Tongue, and the Spirit

PART TWO — THE WITHDRAWALS | *SESSION 3-4*

SESSION 3 — **The Four Horsemen** — 17
Ch 5–7 · Criticism, Contempt, Defensiveness, Stonewalling

SESSION 4 — **Spiritual Weapons** — 20
Ch 8–9 · Spiritual Attacks & Inherited Wounds

PART THREE — THE FIVE DEPOSITS | SESSION 5-6

SESSION 5 — **Honor, Gentleness, Attunement** — 23
Ch 10–12 · Deposits 1, 2 & 3

SESSION 6 — **Repair & Tenderness** — 25
Ch 13–14 · Deposits 4 & 5 · Quick Reference

PART FOUR — THE RESET | SESSION 7-8

SESSION 7 — **The Emotional Audit** — 28
Ch 15 · The Covenant Audit™ · All Five Instruments

SESSION 8 — **The Legacy Ledger** — 30
Ch 16–17 + Epilogue · 30-Day Reset + Legacy Ledger™

The Instruments section contains the 7-Day Emotional Ledger, Ratio Calculator, Four Horsemen Assessment, Eden Standard Safety Assessment, Nervous System Inventory, Daily Five Tracker, and 5:1 Covenant Agreement — all referenced in Chapters 15–16.

Key frameworks used throughout Sacred Deposits. Use as a reference while working through sessions.

Covenant Account™

The marriage as a living ledger, every interaction is a deposit or withdrawal.

Covenant Exchange Rate™

The 5:1 ratio required for a marriage to remain solvent. Below 5:1, the relational balance declines.

The Overdraft Principle™

When withdrawals consistently outpace deposits, the account enters deficit, even in faithful marriages.

Four Horsemen Cascade™

Criticism, contempt, defensiveness, stonewalling, the four patterns that predict relational collapse.

The Daily Five

5 non-negotiable daily deposits: touch, kind word, undivided attention, gratitude, prayer for your spouse.

The Covenant Audit™

Five-instrument assessment that reveals where your account actually stands, not where you wish it stood.

Sacred Breaking

The moment the old pattern becomes intolerable, the prerequisite for reconstruction and change.

Identity Reconstruction

The shift in self-concept required beneath behavior change to make it permanent rather than temporary.

30-Day Reset Protocol™

Four-phase structured protocol for rewiring withdrawal patterns into deposit habits.

The Legacy Ledger™

The intergenerational record of what your covenant is building for the generation watching you build it.

Negative Sentiment Override

When the account is so depleted that even positive deposits are perceived as withdrawals.

Subsidizing Absence™

Physical presence without emotional investment, the most normalized withdrawal in Christian marriage.

The Account

The Covenant Exchange Rate™ — what is building in your marriage and what it costs

> *"Where your treasure is, there your heart will be also."*
>
> — MATTHEW 6:21 (NIV)

Jesus is not making a statement about money. He is making a statement about investment. Where you consistently put your effort, your attention, and your care, that is where your heart follows. This session asks you to look honestly at where your treasure has actually been going.

KEY CONCEPT — THE COVENANT EXCHANGE RATE™

Research conducted over four decades by Dr. John Gottman demonstrates that stable marriages maintain a ratio of at least five positive interactions for every negative one. Below 5:1, the relational balance declines. At 1:1, the marriage enters crisis. Below 1:1, negative sentiment override takes hold — a state where even positive deposits are perceived as withdrawals. Your marriage is not broken. It is overdrawn. And overdrawn accounts can be replenished.

5:1	20:1	1:1
MINIMUM TO SURVIVE	RATIO TO THRIVE	MARRIAGE IN CRISIS

Key frameworks used throughout Sacred Deposits. Use as a reference
while working through sessions.

INDIVIDUAL PREPARATION CHECKLIST

1 Read the Introduction and Chapters 1–2 of Sacred Deposits before this session.

2 Bring one word that honestly describes the current state of your covenant
account. Write it below without overthinking.

3 The book opens with a couple sitting in the third pew — performing together-
ness while an account quietly runs low. Where do you most recognize yourself
in that picture?

4 Estimate your ratio this week. Write significant interactions below, deposits on the
left, withdrawals on the right.

Deposits This Week: **Withdrawals This Week:**

Total: **Total:**

My Estimated Ratio This Week:

Total:

Rate each area as you honestly experience it right now. Not as you hope it is. As it is. Complete individually — do not share until you are in the room together.

AREA		SCALE	
Overall account health	Deficit	1 · 2 · 3 · 4 · 5 · 6 · 7 · 8 · 9 · 10	Thriving
Deposit consistency	Rare	1 · 2 · 3 · 4 · 5 · 6 · 7 · 8 · 9 · 10	Daily
Feeling genuinely valued	Never	1 · 2 · 3 · 4 · 5 · 6 · 7 · 8 · 9 · 10	Always
Emotional safety in conflict	None	1 · 2 · 3 · 4 · 5 · 6 · 7 · 8 · 9 · 10	Complete
Shared sense of investment	One-sided	1 · 2 · 3 · 4 · 5 · 6 · 7 · 8 · 9 · 10	Mutual
Ratio health (gut estimate)	Below 1:1	1 · 2 · 3 · 4 · 5 · 6 · 7 · 8 · 9 · 10	Above 5:1

1. What surprised you most about your own ratings?

2. The most consistent investment I make in this marriage is

The most consistent withdrawal I make, even unintentionally is

These questions are for honest conversation, not performance. You do not have to have answers. You have to be willing to look together.

3 Share your one word. What does your partner's word tell you about their experience of this marriage right now?

4 Where have deposits been most consistent in your marriage? Where have withdrawals been building quietly — the ones no one was counting?

5 What is one withdrawal pattern you have each been making that neither of you has named out loud before tonight?

6 The book says: "Your marriage is not broken. It is overdrawn." Does that fit?
   What does it feel like to call it an overdraft rather than a failure?

7 What would a 5:1 ratio look like in the daily texture of your specific marriage —
   not the concept, the actual behaviors?

8 What is the gap between the account you have right now and the account you are
   trying to build? What is standing in that gap?

These questions are for honest conversation, not performance. You do not have to have answers. You have to be willing to look together.

→ PRACTICE ONE

Ask the currency question

Ask your spouse this week: "What makes you feel most valued by me — specifically?" Listen without defending or explaining. Write their answer below.

→ PRACTICE TWO

Start the 7-day emotional ledger

Turn to Instrument I–1 in the back of this workbook. For seven days, record every significant interaction as a deposit or withdrawal. Do not try to fix anything yet. Just count.

→ PRACTICE THREE

Make one deliberate deposit

Based on what your spouse told you, make one intentional deposit this week. Tell them when you make it.

"We are building a covenant account together. Starting today, we choose to invest with intention."

HIS SIGNATURE   HER SIGNATURE

DATE SIGNED

Emotional Safety

God designed emotional safety — the brain, the tongue, and the spirit in your marriage

"The tongue has the power of life and death, and those who love it will eat its fruit."

— PROVERBS 18:21 (NIV)

Every word you speak deposits or withdrawals. Tone deposits or withdrawals. Chapter 3 establishes that emotional safety was God's original design for intimate relationship. Chapter 4 shows how the brain you were given either defends that design or destroys it.

The Eden Standard

God's original design: fully known and unashamed. The question your marriage must answer: does your spouse feel safe enough to be fully known?

Subsidizing Absence™

Physical presence without emotional investment. Present in the room, withdrawn from the relationship. The most normalized withdrawal in Christian marriage.

The Negativity Tax

Every withdrawal costs 5 deposits minimum. The tax increases when the account is already low. Bad is stronger than good, always, in every measurable domain.

The Polyvagal Ladder

Three states: Ventral Vagal (safe, connected), Sympathetic (fight or flight), Dorsal Vagal (shutdown). Which state does your spouse enter most often around you?

These questions ask about the interior of your marriage — the nervous system, the tone, the things both of you feel but rarely name.

1 On the polyvagal ladder, what state do you most frequently enter during difficult conversations? What does your spouse enter? Where does that mismatch show up most clearly?

2 Where does emotional safety feel most fragile in your marriage — the places where one of you goes quiet, shuts down, or escalates because something feels unsafe?

3 Where has Subsidizing Absence™ appeared in your marriage? Name it without blame.

→ THIS WEEK

The Tone Fast — Seven Days

For seven days, monitor how you say things, not just what you say. Notice your tone before you respond. Record your most important observation.

"We commit to creating emotional safety, not just avoiding conflict, but building the conditions where both of us can be fully known."

HIS SIGNATURE

HER SIGNATURE

DATE SIGNED

II

The Withdrawals

Chapters 5–9 · Sessions 3–4

"The enemy does not always arrive loudly. Sometimes he rides in quietly on a sarcastic tone and a cold shoulder on a Tuesday night."

WHAT PART II COVERS

Part II names the patterns that deplete the covenant account — not the dramatic betrayals that end marriages in crisis, but the consistent withdrawals that hollow them out over years. Chapter 5 introduces the Four Horsemen Cascade™. Chapter 6 gives contempt its own chapter because it deserves one. Chapter 7 names the silent patterns. Chapters 8–9 address spiritual warfare and inherited wounds, the withdrawals that come from outside the couple and from generations before them.

Session Three Covers

Ch 5: The Four Horsemen Enter the Sanctuary
Ch 6: Contempt — The Sin That Grieves the Spirit
Ch 7: The Silent Sins

Session Four Covers

Ch 8: Spiritual Weapons
Ch 9: The Inheritance of Wounds

Your patterns are not destiny. They are data

The Four Horsemen

The Four Horsemen Cascade™ — the patterns that predict relational collapse

"Do not let any unwholesome talk come out of your mouths, but only what is helpful for building others up."

— EPHESIANS 4:29 (NIV)

Paul is not talking about profanity. He is talking about the category of speech that depletes. The Four Horsemen operate in sequence — they do not arrive alone, and they do not leave on their own.

Horseman	Description	Antidote
Criticism	Attacking the person, not the behavior. "You always... you never..." The complaint that became a character indictment.	Self-compassionate complaint: "I feel... when... I need..."
Contempt	Eye-rolls, mockery, dismissiveness. The only Horseman with its own chapter. The strongest single predictor of divorce.	The honor protocol, genuine appreciation and respect.
Defensiveness	Self-protection that says: the problem is you, not me. Takes no responsibility. Blocks repair entirely.	Ownership: "My part in this was..." No defense attached.
Stonewalling	Shutting down, leaving the room, going silent. Nervous system overwhelm masquerading as self-control.	Physiological self-soothing. Take 20 minutes. Return fully.

Deposits This Week:

Withdrawals This Week:

FROM CHAPTER 15 — THE COVENANT AUDIT™

Rate how often you bring each Horseman into your marriage. Not your spouse's score — yours. Honesty here is the first deposit of the repair work.

Horseman	His Frequency	Her Frequency
Criticism	☐ Never	☐ Never
Attacking character, not behavior. "You always / never..."	☐ Rarely	☐ Rarely
	☐ Sometimes	☐ Sometimes
Antidote I will practice:	☐ Often	☐ Often
	☐ Always	☐ Always
Contempt	☐ Never	☐ Never
Eye-rolls, mockery, superiority of tone.	☐ Rarely	☐ Rarely
	☐ Sometimes	☐ Sometimes
Antidote I will practice:	☐ Often	☐ Often
	☐ Always	☐ Always
Defensiveness	☐ Never	☐ Never
Rejecting responsibility. Turning the complaint back	☐ Rarely	☐ Rarely
	☐ Sometimes	☐ Sometimes
Antidote I will practice:	☐ Often	☐ Often
	☐ Always	☐ Always
Stonewalling	☐ Never	☐ Never
Shutting down or leaving during conflict.	☐ Rarely	☐ Rarely
	☐ Sometimes	☐ Sometimes
Antidote I will practice:	☐ Often	☐ Often
	☐ Always	☐ Always

Which horseman costs your account the most? Trace it to its root.

These questions ask you to name the Horsemen that have been riding through your marriage, and to own your part without defense.

1 Share your primary Horseman. What does your pattern look like specifically — the trigger, the behavior, the cost to the account?

2 Where has contempt entered your marriage — even in small forms? A tone. A look. A comment made in front of others. Name it.

3 What cascade — the sequence of Horsemen running in order — do you recognize as the pattern of your hardest arguments?

→ **THIS WEEK**

Interrupt The Cascade Once

When your primary Horseman rises, name it internally, take a 20-minute break, and return with the antidote. Record what happened below.

"We name our Horsemen. We own them without defense. We commit to interrupting the cascade before it runs its course."

HIS SIGNATURE   HER SIGNATURE

DATE SIGNED

Spiritual Weapons & Inherited Wounds

The withdrawals that come from the spiritual realm and from generations before you.

"For our struggle is not against flesh and blood, but against the rulers, against the authorities, against the powers of this dark world."

— EPHESIANS 6:12 (NIV)

Chapter 8 maps the spiritual weapons used against covenants, and the spiritual disciplines that form the counterattack. Chapter 9 names the inheritance of wounds: the patterns from your family of origin that do not stop at the altar.

Spiritual Warfare In Covenant

Ch 8: The enemy targets the covenant account directly.
Disciplines that protect it: prayer, Scripture, Sabbath, the war room. Both partners must be on the same side.

The Inheritance Of Wounds

Ch 9: The patterns from your family of origin migrate into your marriage before you choose them. Awareness is the first antidote. Naming is the second.

My family of origin brought this pattern into my marriage:

The spiritual discipline I need most to protect my covenant right now:

These questions ask you to name the inherited patterns and spiritual pressures shaping your covenant — and to discern where you have been fighting the wrong opponent.

1   What pattern from your family of origin have you imported into this marriage? When did you first recognize it in yourself? How has it affected the account?

2   What spiritual disciplines are protecting your covenant right now? What practices have you let go of that once protected it?

3   Where are you and your spouse most on the same side spiritually? Where are you fighting each other instead of the actual threat to your covenant?

→   THIS WEEK

Pray together for your covenant — once

Not for your spouse to change. For God to strengthen your covenant. Record what shifted — even slightly.

"We are on the same side. We commit to interrupting inherited patterns and protecting our covenant from the weapons aimed at it."

HIS SIGNATURE   HER SIGNATURE

DATE SIGNED

III

The Five Deposits

Chapters 10–14 · Sessions 5–6

THE FIVE SACRED DEPOSITS — QUICK REFERENCE

DEPOSIT 1: **HONOR**	The highest-yield investment in the covenant economy. Private narrative, direct respect, public blessing.
DEPOSIT 2: **GENTLENESS**	The cheapest deposit with the highest return. Tone that keeps the nervous system safe. Strength under control.
DEPOSIT 3: **ATTUNEMENT**	Deep knowing. Love Map intelligence: their current stresses, dreams, fears, and the currency that reaches them.
DEPOSIT 4: **REPENTANCE & REPAIR**	The account restoration mechanism. The Four-Part Apology. Speed of repair is the interest rate on relational debt.
DEPOSIT 5: **CONSISTENT TENDERNESS**	The compound interest your marriage runs on. Small, daily, unremarkable deposits that generate exponential returns.

"Grand gestures are nice. Daily tenderness is wealth."

Honor, Gentleness & Attunement

Deposits 1, 2, and 3 — the first three pillars of the covenant economy

DEPOSIT 1: HONOR — CHAPTER 10

Three dimensions: (1) Private narrative — how you think about your spouse when they are not in the room. (2) Direct respect — how you speak to and about them. (3) Public blessing — how you represent them to others. The highest-yield deposit because it operates simultaneously in all three dimensions.

DEPOSIT 2: GENTLENESS — CHAPTER 11

The Gentle Startup: "I feel… when… I need…" instead of "You always… you never…" Conversations that begin with a harsh startup end badly 96% of the time. Gentleness is not weakness. It is strength operating without the need to dominate. The cheapest deposit with the highest return.

DEPOSIT 3: ATTUNEMENT — CHAPTER 12

Love Map intelligence: your spouse's current stresses, dreams, fears, and the currency that reaches them right now. Couples who turn toward bids for connection 86% of the time stay together. Those at 33% do not. Deposit in their denomination, not yours.

Most Natural Deposit For Me

Deposit That Costs Me The Most

These questions ask you to look honestly at where honor, gentleness, and attunement are most missing — and where their presence would most change the account.

1   Where is Honor most missing in your private narrative — the thoughts you carry about your spouse when they are not in the room? What does your internal broadcast actually say?

2   Where has a harsh startup — in tone, timing, or word choice — cost the account most in your marriage? What would a gentle startup have looked like in that specific moment?

3   What is a bid for connection your spouse makes regularly that you have been missing? What would turning toward it look like this week?

→   THIS WEEK

The Honor Protocol — Three Acts

One act of private honor (adjust your internal narrative), one act of direct respect (name something specific they did), one act of public blessing (represent them well to someone else).

"We commit to depositing in honor, gentleness, and attunement — not when convenient, but as the consistent posture of this covenant."

HIS SIGNATURE   HER SIGNATURE

DATE SIGNED

Repair & Tenderness

Deposits 4 and 5 — the Four-Part Apology and the compound interest of daily care

---

DEPOSIT 4: REPENTANCE & REPAIR — CHAPTER 13

The Four-Part Apology — what full repair actually requires:

1 ACKNOWLEDGE THE HARM

Name exactly what you did. Not the category — the specific act.

2 ACCEPT RESPONSIBILITY

No "but I was also hurt." Own it without defense attached.

3 EXPRESS EMPATHY

Name what it cost them. "I understand this made you feel..."

4 COMMIT TO CHANGE

Name the specific behavior you are changing — not a vague aspiration.

DEPOSIT 5: CONSISTENT TENDERNESS — CHAPTER 14

The Daily Five — non-negotiable, daily, regardless of mood:

One touch · One kind word · One moment of undivided attention · One expression of gratitude · One prayer for your spouse

Grand gestures are nice. Daily tenderness is wealth. The compound interest on small, consistent deposits over a lifetime is the most powerful force in a covenant account.

One incomplete repair I need to return to:

1   The book says "Speed of repair is the interest rate on relational debt." Where has delayed repair compounded — a rupture acknowledged but never fully repaired? Name it.

2   Which part of the Four-Part Apology stalls most consistently in your repairs — naming the harm, owning it, expressing empathy, or committing to change?

3   Which of the Daily Five is most consistently missing in your marriage right now? What would it feel like in the account if it were present every single day for 30 days?

→   THIS WEEK

Begin The Daily Five — Seven Days

Start the Daily Five Tracker (Instrument I–5) this week. All five deposits. Every day. Track consistency and note what shifts in the account by Day 7.

"We commit to full repair — not just apology. And to the daily tenderness that compounds into covenant wealth over a lifetime."

HIS SIGNATURE   HER SIGNATURE

DATE SIGNED

IV

The Reset

Chapters 15–17 · Sessions 7–8

"You cannot fix what you refuse to count. And the courage to count honestly is the first deposit of the reset."

WHAT PART IV CONTAINS

Chapter 15 is the audit — five instruments that reveal where your covenant actually stands. Chapter 16 is the 30-Day Reset Protocol: four phases, one month, the neural pathway work required to make change permanent. Chapter 17 is the legacy — what you are building for the generation watching you build it. All five audit instruments are reproduced in full in the Instruments section of this workbook.

Session Seven Covers

Ch 15: The Covenant Audit™ Complete all five instruments before this session. Bring your results to discuss together as an act of honest confession.

Session Eight Covers

Ch 16–17: 30-Day Reset Protocol + The Legacy Ledger™ Identity Reconstruction. The 5:1 Covenant Agreement.
The legacy you pass on.

The Emotional Audit

The Covenant Audit™ — five instruments, one honest account balance

"Examine yourselves, to see whether you are in the faith. Test yourselves."

— 2 CORINTHIANS 13:5 (NIV)

The Covenant Audit™ uses five instruments to reveal the honest state of your account. You cannot repair what you refuse to measure. This is the moment the system asks you to count — accurately, without flinching, what has actually been building in your marriage.

THE FIVE INSTRUMENTS — COMPLETE IN INSTRUMENTS SECTION BEFORE THIS SESSION

1 THE 7-DAY EMOTIONAL LEDGER

Track every significant interaction for 7 days. Deposit or withdrawal. Count daily. This is your baseline ratio.

2 THE RATIO CALCULATOR

Estimate your ratio across 8 relational contexts against Gottman benchmarks.

3 FOUR HORSEMEN FREQUENCY SCORE

Rate how often each Horseman appears in your own behavior. Trace each to its root.

4 EDEN STANDARD SAFETY ASSESSMENT

Rate emotional safety across 5 dimensions: predictability, vulnerability tolerance, conflict safety, physical safety of touch, and spiritual transparency.

5 NERVOUS SYSTEM STATE INVENTORY

Using the polyvagal ladder, identify which state you enter most often around your spouse — and which state your spouse enters most often around you.

→ Complete all five instruments before Session 7. Bring your results to share together as an act of confession.

Share your audit results as confession — not as ammunition or evidence. "This is what I saw in myself." No defense. No rebuttal. Just honest reporting.

1 What did your 7-Day Ratio reveal that surprised you most? Where were you overestimating your deposits or underestimating your withdrawals?

2 Which of the eight ratio contexts scored lowest? What is specifically driving that context — and what would change it?

3 What did the Eden Standard Safety Assessment reveal about where your spouse does not yet feel fully safe? What is the one specific thing that would raise their lowest score?

→ **THIS WEEK**

Begin the 30-Day Reset — Phase One: Awareness

Observe and record. Use the 7-Day Ledger as your reset baseline. Do not fix anything yet. On Day 7, share your findings as confession.

"We have looked at the balance honestly. We are choosing repair over denial. The 30-Day Reset begins now."

HIS SIGNATURE   HER SIGNATURE

DATE SIGNED

The 30-Day Reset & The Legacy Ledger

The 30-Day Reset Protocol™ + The Legacy Ledger™

Chapter 16 lays out the 30-Day Reset Protocol™ — the four-phase sequence that rewires withdrawal patterns into deposit habits. Chapter 17 turns the lens outward: your covenant is not a private project. It is the pattern someone is inheriting.

THE 30-DAY RESET — FOUR PHASES

PHASE ONE — DAYS 1–7:
AWARENESS

Track every significant interaction for 7 days. Deposit or withdrawal. Count daily. This is your baseline ratio.

PHASE TWO — DAYS 8–14:
ELIMINATION

Remove the heaviest withdrawals. Identify your primary Horseman. Begin the Tone Fast.

PHASE THREE — DAYS 15–21:
INVESTMENT

One deposit per day. Mon: Honor. Tue: Gentleness. Wed: Attunement. Thu: Repair. Fri: Tenderness.

PHASE FOUR — DAYS 22–30:
INTEGRATION

Build infrastructure: Daily Five, Weekly Check-In, Repair Phrase Library, 5:1 Covenant Agreement.

THE LEGACY LEDGER™ — CHAPTER 17

What you are building is not just for you. The boy on the top stair, listening through the floor — he does not hear the words. He hears the pattern. The geometry of your marriage becomes the architecture of his future relationships. The Legacy Ledger asks: what are you passing on? And is it what you intend to pass?

Identity reconstruction — who am I choosing to become in this marriage?

Rate your covenant account today. Compare to your Session One scores. The movement is the evidence of investment.

AREA	S1 His	S8 His	SCALE	S1 Her	S8 Her
Overall account health	______	______	1 · 2 · 3 · 4 · 5 · 6 · 7 · 8 · 9 · 10	______	______
Deposit consistency	______	______	1 · 2 · 3 · 4 · 5 · 6 · 7 · 8 · 9 · 10	______	______
Currency intelligence	______	______	1 · 2 · 3 · 4 · 5 · 6 · 7 · 8 · 9 · 10	______	______
Five deposits funded	______	______	1 · 2 · 3 · 4 · 5 · 6 · 7 · 8 · 9 · 10	______	______
Withdrawal patterns managed	______	______	1 · 2 · 3 · 4 · 5 · 6 · 7 · 8 · 9 · 10	______	______
Repair standard	______	______	1 · 2 · 3 · 4 · 5 · 6 · 7 · 8 · 9 · 10	______	______
Hard season capacity	______	______	1 · 2 · 3 · 4 · 5 · 6 · 7 · 8 · 9 · 10	______	______
Legacy confidence	______	______	1 · 2 · 3 · 4 · 5 · 6 · 7 · 8 · 9 · 10	______	______

What moved most since Session One?

What still needs the most work?

Our Covenant Investment Statement

Written together. Signed. Dated. Kept.

The account we are building will be characterized by:

"The eight sessions end. The investment does not.
We are building something that outlasts every season we build it through."

HIS SIGNATURE

HER SIGNATURE

DATE SIGNED

The Investment Continues

The program ends. The investment does not.

→ BEGIN WEEK 1 OF THE COVENANT JOURNAL

The 52-week journal hands off directly from this eight-week workbook. The class ends. The covenant does not.

→ TAKE THE SACRED DEPOSITS ASSESSMENT

Visit eggenix.com/sacred to receive your Covenant Wealth Score™ and identify your highest-impact deposit opportunities.

→ REVISIT YOUR EIGHT DECLARATIONS TOGETHER

At your six-month and one-year anniversaries, read your Covenant Declarations aloud. Measure the distance traveled.

→ INTRODUCE ANOTHER COUPLE TO THE SYSTEM

Teaching what you have learned is the highest form of deposit. The legacy of this work extends beyond your own account.

Additional notes:

Assessment & Tracking Tools

Chapters 15–16 call for these instruments by name

Complete the instruments before Session 7 discussion. The manuscript explicitly states: "The companion workbook contains the complete audit instruments."

CONTENTS OF THIS SECTION

I–1 THE 7-DAY EMOTIONAL LEDGER

7 days of interaction tracking. Your baseline ratio. Referenced throughout Chapter 15.

I–2 THE RATIO CALCULATOR

Your ratio across 8 relational contexts against Gottman benchmarks.

I–3 EDEN STANDARD SAFETY ASSESSMENT

Emotional safety across 5 dimensions — His and Her scores compared.

I–4 NERVOUS SYSTEM STATE INVENTORY

Which polyvagal state you enter most often around your spouse.

I–5 DAILY FIVE TRACKER

30-day tracking grid for the five non-negotiable daily deposits.

I–6 5:1 COVENANT AGREEMENT

Your shared commitments, repair phrases, and daily rituals, written and signed.

Referenced in Chapter 15 — Complete Before Session 7

For 7 days, record every significant interaction. W (Withdrawal) or Mark D (Deposit). Count your daily totals. Most people overestimate deposits and underestimate withdrawals. The ledger does not lie.

Day 1   Withdrawal   Deposit

☐ W   ☐ D

☐ W   ☐ D

☐ W   ☐ D

Deposits _____   Withdrawals _____   Today's ratio _____ : 1

Day 2   Withdrawal   Deposit

☐ W   ☐ D

☐ W   ☐ D

☐ W   ☐ D

Deposits _____   Withdrawals _____   Today's ratio _____ : 1

Day 3   Withdrawal   Deposit

☐ W   ☐ D

☐ W   ☐ D

☐ W   ☐ D

Deposits _____   Withdrawals _____   Today's ratio _____ : 1

Day 4   Withdrawal   Deposit

☐ W   ☐ D

☐ W   ☐ D

☐ W   ☐ D

Deposits _____   Withdrawals _____   Today's ratio _____ : 1

Day 5	Withdrawal	Deposit
	☐ W	☐ D
	☐ W	☐ D
	☐ W	☐ D

Deposits _____   Withdrawals _____   Today's ratio _____ : 1

Day 6	Withdrawal	Deposit
	☐ W	☐ D
	☐ W	☐ D
	☐ W	☐ D

Deposits _____   Withdrawals _____   Today's ratio _____ : 1

Day 7	Withdrawal	Deposit
	☐ W	☐ D
	☐ W	☐ D
	☐ W	☐ D

Deposits _____   Withdrawals _____   Today's ratio _____ : 1

7-DAY TOTALS

Total Deposits _____   Total Withdrawals _____   7-Day ratio _____ : 1   5:1 Gottman benchmark

What surprised you most about your ratio?

____

____

____

Estimate your positive-to-negative ratio across these eight contexts.
Gottman benchmarks: **5:1** during conflict = **Healthy.**
20:1 in daily life = **Thriving.** Below **1:1** = **Negative** sentiment override.

Context	His ratio	Her ratio
During Conflict Benchmark: 5:1		
Weekday Evening Benchmark: 20:1		
Weekends Together Benchmark: 20:1		
Around the Children Benchmark: 20:1		
In Public / Social Settings Benchmark: 20:1		
During Intimacy Benchmark: 20:1		
About Finances Benchmark: 5:1		
In Spiritual Life Together Benchmark: 20:1		

Where is your lowest ratio? What is driving it?

Rate how safe you feel across the five dimensions of emotional safety. Complete individually. The gap between your scores and your spouse's scores are where the most important conversations need to happen.

Safety Dimension	HIS	SCALE	S1 Her
Predictability I can predict how my spouse will respond — I am not walking on eggshells.		1 · 2 · 3 · 4 · 5 · 6 · 7 · 8 · 9 · 10	
Vulnerability Tolerance I can be weak, sad, or afraid around my spouse without being judged or dismissed.		1 · 2 · 3 · 4 · 5 · 6 · 7 · 8 · 9 · 10	
Conflict Safety Disagreements do not feel dangerous — they do not end in contempt or shutdown.		1 · 2 · 3 · 4 · 5 · 6 · 7 · 8 · 9 · 10	
Physical Safety of Touch Touch from my spouse communicates care, not transaction or demand.		1 · 2 · 3 · 4 · 5 · 6 · 7 · 8 · 9 · 10	
Spiritual Transparency I can share my faith, my doubt, and my prayers with my spouse without shame.		1 · 2 · 3 · 4 · 5 · 6 · 7 · 8 · 9 · 10	

Biggest gap between your scores?

What would raise your lowest score by 2 points?

Using the polyvagal ladder, identify which state you most frequently enter during interactions with your spouse. This tells you where safety is — and where it is not.

Ventral vagal	Sympathetic	Dorsal vagal
Safe & Connected	**Fight Or Flight**	**Shutdown**
Open, curious, warm, present. The state where deposits land and love is felt. This is God's design.	Read together. Share answers as confession, not accusation. Begin the 30-Day Reset at Chapter 15.	Collapsed, disconnected. The account is shut down entirely. Neither deposit nor withdrawal registers.
Engaged listening	Defensiveness rises	Goes silent or leaves room
Playfulness & humor	Voice volume increases	Flat affect minimal response
Ease in conflict	Elevated heart rate	Emotional numbness
Physical closeness comfortable	Criticism or contempt appears	Difficulty accessing words
Genuine curiosity about spouse	Need to win the exchange	Feels gone while present

The state I enter most often around my spouse:

The state my spouse enters most often:

What triggers my shift out of ventral vagal:

What I can do to keep my spouse in ventral vagal:

**Five non-negotiable deposits. Every day. Regardless of mood.
Grand gestures are nice. Daily tenderness is wealth.**

1   **ONE TOUCH**

Physical contact communicating tenderness, not transaction.

2   **ONE KIND WORD**

Specific, genuine, not flattery.

3   **UNDIVIDED ATTENTION**

Phone down. Eyes up. One uninterrupted moment.

4   **GRATITUDE**

For the small thing, not the grand one.

5   **PRAYER FOR YOUR SPOUSE**

Silent or spoken. Ask God to bless them.

30-DAY TRACKING GRID — CHECK OFF EACH DAY YOU COMPLETED ALL FIVE

Week 1

Week 2

Week 3

Week 4

End of 30 days — what shifted in the account?

**Required between phase three and phase four of the 30-day reset
"Behavioral change without identity change is temporary. The protocol asks you to name who you are becoming, not just what you are doing differently."**

DEPOSIT 4: INTEGRATION — CHAPTER 16

Complete individually. Then share with your spouse. Identity proclaimed in the presence of a witness becomes covenant.

Who was I in this marriage before the reset?

Who am I choosing to become?

The specific pattern I am leaving behind — and the identity I am choosing instead: "I was the one who stonewalled. I am becoming the one who stays present when it is hard."

I am becoming:

Our 5:1 Covenant Agreement

Written together. Signed. Posted. Lived from.

Our primary deposits — the investments we are committing to:

Our withdrawal patterns — named and interrupted:

Our repair phrases — what we say when we need to restore:

Our weekly ritual — how we protect the account each week:

Our daily five commitment:

"Therefore what God has joined together, let no one separate"

— MARK 10:9 (NIV)

The Covenant Agreement

We commit to stewarding the covenant entrusted to us. We will protect the exchange rate of our marriage. We will practice honor, gentleness, attunement, repair, and tenderness. We will invest daily in the emotional wealth of our home. We will audit honestly, repair quickly, and build what we want our children to inherit.

One deposit at a time. Five to one.
Built, not downloaded. Starting now.

____

SIGNATURE

____

SIGNATURE

____

PRINTED NAME

____

PRINTED NAME

____

DATE SIGNED

EQGENIX INC.